THE 2020 REMOTE WORK GUIDE

-

HOW TO WORK FROM HOME AND MAKE MONEY IN 2020

Copyright © 2020- All Rights Reserved

This book is copyright protected, and is intended for personal use only.

No parts of this publication may be reproduced in any form or by any means, including printing, scanning, photocopying, or otherwise unless explicitly stated. Any attempts to amend, sell, distribute, paraphrase, or quote the contents of this book, without the consent of the author or copyright owner can and will result in legal action.

Please note that the details included within this book are for informational purposes only. The publisher and author have made every effort to ensure the accuracy of the information contained within this book. However, they make no warranties as to the completeness of the contents herein, and hence hereby declaim any liability for errors, omissions, or contrary interpretation of the subject matter.

Disclaimer

The information contained cannot be considered a substitute for treatment as prescribed by a therapist or other professional. By reading this book, you are assuming all risks associated with using the advice, data, and suggestions given below, with a full understanding that you, solely, are responsible for anything that may occur as a result of putting this information into action in any way – regardless of your interpretation of the advice.

TABLE OF CONTENTS

INTRODUCTION 1

CHAPTER ONE: WHAT ARE REMOTE JOBS 6

CHAPTER TWO: BEST REMOTE JOBS PLATFORMS IN 2020 21

CHAPTER THREE: REMOTE JOBS WITH THE BEST PAY IN 2020 30

CHAPTER FOUR: BECOMING A SUCCESSFUL REMOTE WORKER IN 2020 44

CHAPTER FIVE: KNOWING WHAT REMOTE EMPLOYERS WANT 52

CHAPTER SIX: CRAFTING YOUR RESUME FOR A REMOTE JOB 58

CONCLUSION 62

INTRODUCTION

Ordinarily, people who are on the look-out to earn extra cash are often advised to take a part-time job or hustle such as working as a hotel attendant, a counter assistant at a restaurant, amongst all other posts. However, most of these persons do not have the requisite energy or time to invest so as to perform optimally in these kinds of jobs. Should we talk about the student who leaves school late and still has to catch us with posts at restaurants? Or a working-class parent with kids to cater for and bills to pay doing two or three jobs? For persons like these, taking two to three side jobs or part-time hustles might be an excruciating experience for them.

Therefore, there is an immense need for people that fall under the categories highlighted above, to find part-time jobs which are stress-free and guarantee cash at the end of the day. This is where remote jobs fit in. Since the onset of the Internet, the idea of earning with little stress has been pioneered. People can work from anywhere in the world in the comfort of their rooms and of course – at their own leisure. One is not discouraged by proximity, a pre-planned schedule or office hour life. In addition, there is the benefit of not having to sit in long boring office meetings.

Interestingly, you can also earn via working on activities that you love or consider as your hobby. For instance, remote jobs can afford a person who loves making graphic designs the opportunity of sitting in the comfort and confines of his homes to create visual designs for a client and earn a lot of money while doing the same. Sitting in my room and earning via activities that are my hobbies? Wow! I guess that's the most exciting you have heard in 2020, right? Of course! Understandably, for every human – there is this unexplainable level of excitement that comes from relaxing in your comfort zone while making a lot of cash comfortably.

Another alluring fact is, you can work at your own leisure, and with your own schedule. This is better than working around the clock with annoying or unpleasant co-workers – who sometimes interrupt your day with the company gossip that you most times don't give two hoots about. If you're someone like myself – who doesn't take the slightest delight in long and tedious meetings – this book is an eye-opener to a huge discovery that will completely liberate you. Self-employment at its best – is what this book is about to open your eyes to.

In this book, readers would also learn how to craft a creative resume that will land you your desired remote jobs. Asides that, this book would also expose readers to skills that remote companies always look-out for in remote job seekers.

Also, this book is not restricted to just one field; Everyone from all walks of life are guaranteed one remote job or another that works for them because when it comes remote jobs – there is something for everyone.

Now, you are probably thinking within yourself: "what

are the kinds of remote jobs I can do in my comfort zone?" The answer to this kind of question and many more questions at the back of your mind is what this book intends to provide for. Additionally, this book would also discuss how to make money off these remote jobs. Sit back and enjoy. Happy Reading!

CHAPTER ONE: WHAT ARE REMOTE JOBS

As the standards of living get higher and well-paying jobs become scarce, it has become necessary to look for other jobs from which you can make money from without stressing yourself up or wearing yourself out. This is where remote jobs come in. With the need to look for extra cash and jobs that can earn you that extra cash from the comfort of your home, more and more remote jobs keep popping up by the minute and now everybody including students, can do one thing or the other and earn some money without affecting their schoolwork or other activities.

Remote works are jobs that you can do away from the

office, and from the comfort of anywhere you are. It could be from home, at a café, a park, a plane, or as you take a leisurely walk. Remote work is also a style of working which allows professionals to work outside the typical office environment. Remote work denounces the traditional belief that all-important jobs can only be done from the office as it provides a professional with the flexibility of working while still completing jobs and working as optimally as a person who does all his jobs in an office. Amazing right? With remote works, you are not confined to the typical 9 -5 office hours. Instead, you are allowed to choose what time and place work best for you thereby enabling you to get the best from your professional life as well as your personal life because how you work is solely in your hands.

UNDERSTANDING HOW REMOTE JOBS WORK

For some, the definition of remote working is solely freelancing jobs. Well, at a time, it was like that. However, in recent times, the dynamics have changed. In our technologically advanced society, remote works are on the rise, and a person can find themselves making money even as they sleep at night. This is where the beauty of remote work lies; you are given numerous choices and allowed to pick which one works best for you at any given point. You can decide to take a job which requires you to be in the office at least once a week, and you can also choose a job which does not require you to appear in an office at all as long as you do the job that needs to be done. If you are working a full-time office job which you do not want to quit but at the same time you want to start working remotely, remote work gives you the opportunity to utilize "co-working spaces" which allows you to balance your professional working life, with your remote work without any strain in you. Let me give a brief explanation of what co-working space is.

Co-working is an arrangement between different employees from different companies in which they agree to use an office space together and share in its expenses. Co-working spaces have become more popular following the rise of remote jobs because they allow for effective resource management by reducing cost as a result of the sharing of infrastructure and available amenities. It also gives you a professional setting in which you can meet clients instead of meeting them at the coffee shop or the park. Co-working spaces are places that allow you to connect with different people working in different companies and sectors of society. It also allows you to make use of the information and knowledge available to others, which you do not have at no extra cost to you.

Coming back to remote work, we were talking about how freelancing jobs are not the only means you can earn money as there are now a lot of remote works from which you can make money from. As amazing as that is, the most crucial question is, does remote work pay as much as an office job? With an office job, you are assured of a steady salary and a possible increase in it depending on how high you go in your place of work, but can remote works guarantee you a regular salary as well as stability? When remote work first came on the scene, professionals who subscribed to it and used it were paid less because employers believed that they did not face the same challenges as someone who came to work every day. But as clamors for equality in pay for both remote workers and office workers increased, remote workers are now finding themselves earning as much or almost as much as an office worker. Some professions, at the moment, pay remote workers as much as office workers or even more as the case may be. For instance, developers who work outside the office environment, are paid as much as their office counterparts and in some cases, even more than their peers who go to the office. Maybe this is because no one can deny the steady rise and popularity which remote works seem to be getting. A study conducted from 2005 to 2015 showed that remote work steadily increased in the period of ten years by 115%, and the number of professionals doing remote jobs went up from 1.8 million to 3.9 million and counting. As more people find pleasure in working remotely, they also find that the cost of transportation to and from work, as well as the expenses that would have been spent at the office in a day, are now saved up and put into other profitable ventures. Despite the fact that remote workers are now getting paid as equally as office workers, there are still some professions in which the difference cannot be bridged, and there are others that are very profitable and rewarding for remote workers. These professions will be discussed in the next chapter, but for now, let us go to the benefits of remote working.

BENEFITS OF REMOTE WORKING

The only reason why working remotely is becoming popular and growing steadily is because of the numerous benefits which it offers. The first and probably the most popular benefit is the flexibility of working hours, which remote work allows professionals to have. There is this sweet joy and pleasure of not being confined to work within a time frame and to be able to work at your convenience while still working optimally. For some people, this is perhaps the only reason why they chose working remotely over working in an office; the opportunity to be free and dictate your own pace.

Another benefit of remote working is that it reduces the stress of having to commute to work every single day. Just think of how nice it is not to have to rush to catch the bus or worry about being late to the office because you do not have to go to the office. Commuting from home to the office and back for most professionals can be very tiring and time-wasting, especially when you consider unforeseen circumstances such as traffic. Also, being able to work from the comfort of wherever you are, allows you to save up the money that you would have used for commuting and put it into something profitable or can instead be spent on things that you love.

Small businesses can in no way compete with larger businesses and companies in the area of salaries and additional benefits. By this, they find themselves losing valuable employees who are looking for greener pastures, to larger companies who can offer them what they are looking for. As such, one of the ways these smaller businesses can have the edge over larger businesses is by giving its employees the freedom that comes with remote work and by offering their employees such freedom to take care of their personal life without affecting their professional lives. Remote work allows these small businesses to retain their employees as well as increase productivity and efficiency since the employees are happy and are dedicated to their jobs. Also, as a result of the growth of social media and technological advancement, the present generation has become accustomed to being able to communicate with people all over the world as well as communicate effectively from anywhere they are and, as such, expects the same from their workplace. Employers who grant their employees and future employees the ease of communicating wherever they find that they have more people willing to work for them than other employers who follow the traditional office way. Also, by allowing their employees to work remotely, employers and businesses can hire qualified personnel that does not live close by which can be very beneficial and helpful in the growth of small businesses.

As earlier said, remote working allows for lower costs of operation not just for employees, but for employers as well. Getting office space is expensive, and the more employees you have, the more office space you need which means spending more money than necessary but by allowing remote working, an employer can reduce the amount of office space required as employees do not have to come to the office all the time. By embracing the flexibility that comes with remote working, businesses are also increasing the productivity and amount of output that their employees can put out. According to a survey conducted in Canada, it was found that the productivity of homeworkers ranked higher than the productivity of those that worked from the office because they are not distracted by their co-workers or their working place plus, it reduces the amount of competition between co-workers because everyone is working in their own pace and level.

For employees, remote working allows them to balance their work-life with their personal life, especially those who have families to cater to. As much as you want to give your best to your jobs, you also want to be there when your kids need you and not be an absentee parent. Remote working allows you to go about your everyday life while your work-life does not suffer from it. When you look at it, when millions of people do not have to go to work every day before they can get jobs done, it also benefits the environment. The fumes from our vehicles as we go to and from work, pollute our environment and by cutting it down a bit, we in no small measure, contribute to the protection of our environment. According to a report on the " State of telecommuting in the United States employee workforce" remote working, has helped to take over 600,000 cars off the road as a result of millions of people being able to work from the comfort of their homes which subsequently, has helped to reduced greenhouse gas emissions. As over a million tons of greenhouse gasses are avoided each year, oil savings have gone up to about 900 million dollars as well, which helps in sustaining the economy.

Since employees are given time for themselves, they are happier, and since they do not have to rush to the office every morning, they can focus more on their health and have the time to make good health choices as well as engage in more physical activities. Employees have been known to collapse from stress, and not being capable of doing anything else when they come back from work, and remote working helps to correct that problem as a result of the freedom which employees possess.

As you can see, remote working is going nowhere as more and more people are opting to make use of it instead of going to the office every day. Even full-time employees can take a breather once in a while and benefit from the opportunities remote working presents. It is beneficial for both employers and employers as well as large businesses and small ones so, it will be no surprise when in the coming years, remote working becomes the most popular thing around.

CHAPTER TWO: BEST REMOTE JOBS PLATFORMS IN 2020

As remote work becomes more popular, the platforms available for it grows as well. There are as many worksites as there are jobs, but some still stand out among the others as the best worksite, a remote worker can get jobs from. Such work websites include:

▫ Flexjobs: this network offers full-time, part-time, and even some remote jobs are the perfect start for someone just venturing into the remote job world. Remote companies come on flex job websites and post jobs for free, but remote workers have to pay roughly 15 dollars monthly to become a premium user. Candidly, the monthly subscription is a ridiculous sum of money when compared to the full range of job opportunities posted by the website. Outside the world of paid client and customer service relationship, the site also provides a voluminous amount of resources for job seekers. Another factor that stands this website out is that – unlike other networks who majorly post jobs in the tech industry, flex job posts job from arguably every walks of life.

• Hubstaff Talent: on this network, you have the choice of searching for remote jobs that are full time, hourly freelance contracts, and even jobs with a fixed price. So if you are looking to make remote jobs a passive source of income, this website is exceptionally made for you. Hubstaff Talents deals in remote jobs such as web development, social media marketing, graphics designing, customer services, 3D animations, etc.

Remote.com: This site gives users a wide range of access to jobs that match their profile description. Consequently, creating a profile is an essential feature on this website. This network also has a premium option which gives additional exposure to users. This premium option cost $19. Another striking feature of Remote.com is that they allow you to see the remuneration for a job before you apply. Remote.com also post new jobs almost every day.

 Remote.co: although a subsidiary of flex job, is a network that also offers remote job posting. They post daily, and they post jobs with good pay. They have great blog resources, and it is a great place to learn a lot about working remotely.

 WeWorkRemotely: this is solely a job board – an incredible job for remote workers. On this website, there are no application or registration fees for premium options. Another interesting fact is, their website is easy to navigate as it has little or no complications. The interface of the website is easily accessible by anyone. However, most jobs on this network are focused on software engineering and design. Nonetheless, when searching for a remote job, WeWorkRemotely, is a go-to site for me.

⦁ AngelList: unlike other remote jobs website, this remote job website is specifically set up for start-ups. If you are interested in start-up businesses, then this is the website for you. There is no cost to use AngelList, but you must create a profile. Your profile is your selling point on this network; hence, there is an imperative need to make your profile catchy and outstanding. Simply, your profile is more or less like your resume. Clients carefully peruse the profile of users before they give them jobs. There are no premium fees, and new jobs are often uploaded on a daily bases. You get interviewed by bidding for jobs. To bid, you have to – click "yes, I'm interested" and by leaving a small note for the hiring manager. If the remote job company likes your profile, they will set up an interview with you. Upon passing the interview, you instantaneously get the job. The process with AngelList is pretty straightforward and uncomplicated, no resume or cover letter needed as your AngelList profile already serves this purpose. Another striking feature on AngelList is that you can apply for a job and receive a response from the remote job company within a few hours. Also, AngelList shows you if a job posting is still active or not.

• Pangian: becoming a user on Pangian means you are tapping into one of the fastest-growing online communities for not only finding remote jobs to sign up for, but also for connecting with fellow remote workers based in over 120 countries from around the globe. The website boasts of over 12,000 job postings from over 300 remote job companies. The website most unique feature is how it serves as a community and chat forums where you can meet with fellow remote workers and learn from one another. Users also share remote jobs tips. Pangian also serves as a nexus for a remote worker to connect and learn from one another.

• Jobspresso: this website is your go-to site for your daily job posting. They have postings from the biggest names in the remote work industry, and they post the jobs on a daily basis. I, for one particularly love Jobspresso just because they post high-quality jobs with good pays, and they publish these jobs every day. Following Jobspresso on their social media outlet is an excellent way to monitor their job postings.

BEST REMOTE WORK COMPANIES AROUND

Also, as remote work may seem very difficult to get, there are go-to companies available for remote job seekers to apply to. There are as many companies as there are jobs, but some still stand out among the others as the best platforms, a remote worker can work on. Vividly, I would be discussing some of these companies in the foregoing paragraphs.

One of these companies is Aspen, which is regarded as the best remote company around. The headquarters is in Australia, and it provides technological services. Companies like Kelly Services and Williams-Sonoma are also among the list of top ten remote work companies because, as of 2019, they posted the highest number of remote jobs. Some companies that have been leading the way for the past 5 to 6 years include CVS Health, Kaplan, Appen, Dell, Humana, and American Express. New companies like World Travel Holdings and Achieve Test Prep, were at 2019, also at the top of the list.

Although you can work on your own, it is advisable that as someone just starting, you should attach yourself to one of these companies or any other known to you since these companies have been tried and trusted, and therefore, it will be easier for you to pick up jobs there. After a while of working in these companies, learning the ropes, and acquiring clients of your own, you can them leave and spread your wings as wide as you can since you can now stand on your own.

CHAPTER THREE: REMOTE JOBS WITH THE BEST PAY IN 2020

Tanveer Sahail once said: "making money is very simple but not easy." I would like to re-phrase that and say: "making money via remote job is simple but not easy." For emphasis purposes, I would like to reiterate that the emergence and development of the internet led to a huge surge of jobs you can do remotely from your comfort zone. Whether that's working remotely for a particular firm, industry or company, or you are starting your own business, there is an over-abundance of work-from-home opportunities available on the internet. In this chapter, many of such opportunities would be expounded upon in foregoing paragraphs, kindly follow closely and attentively.

1. **Affiliate Marketing**: this is a referral marketing system where you can easily earn a commission via referral. Affiliate marketing is one of the most basic means to add an existing income stream to your business. The main task of an affiliate marketer is traffic generation. You are solely tasked with a responsibility: promoting the use of the affiliate link on your website or blog. The more users that click the link, the more money you earn. If you are financially strong, you can direct traffic even faster with paid advertising methods, which include: paid ads on Facebook and using Google Ad words. Note, however – free traffic is a great idea; however, once you have the resources, you should commence the use of paid ads to promote and enhance your business quickly and swiftly. There is

various numerous affiliate network. One of the most popular ones is ClickBank, which is one of the oldest and most popular affiliate networks. ClickBank is a billion-dollar digital company that specializes in digital products like e-books and software, as well as membership sites. As an affiliate with ClickBank, you have to put up their affiliate link on your website or blog site, and the more traffic you generate via the link, the more the commission you earn. Also, another popular affiliate marketing network is Amazon. As you may already know, Amazon is a large market hub that sells almost anything and everything in the world – physical and digital products inclusive. As an Amazon Associate, you earn more commission on traffic generated for the digital product than you would earn when you generate the same for a physical product.

More importantly, every affiliate – individual or network affiliates or associates should indulge in selling digital products – that is where loads of money is.

2. **Blogging**: This is closely related to what I discussed above. The only difference is, affiliates earn while they generate traffic for some other network or person while bloggers generate traffics for their sites. Blogging is cheap and cost-friendly. It is just the same way you write about your favorite place, music or food in your jotting pad. But this time, you are writing about your favorite things on your site, and eventually, you can start making money from your site. You can make money either by generating traffic on your blog site or by putting up an advert for a person or company and charging them for same.

3. **Copywriting**: by now, you must have heard from every tom, dick and harry that copywriting is a great way to earn money as you travel the world. In a research recently concluded, it was observed that freelance copywriters make as much $30,000 – $100, 000. However, it varies – whilst new copywriter with minimum experience and copywriting skills earn $3,000 – $15, 000 per year. In contrast, medium and top writers with a premium experience and copywriting skills will earn the price as mentioned earlier. Interestingly, a freelance copywriter can work as many jobs as he can handle. As the more the jobs he takes, the more he earns. To earn as a copywriter, you can easily apply to a Freelance network that connects the client and the freelance copywriter. Such freelancing websites include but are not restricted to

Upwork, Fiverr and Guru. To earn better, you've to pick a niche and develop yourself. The more experience you get, the fatter your earnings get. Also, getting licenses and certifications project your skills to the clients. Commonly, more skills mean more money.

4. **Software engineering**: nowadays, there is an insatiable urge for useful and distinctive software. The world keeps evolving, and it is evident that everyone is turning in the direction of the Computer and internet. Your software could be an application on an IOS device or an Android device as long as it tackles and solves a particular human problem – you can massively earn a lot of fortune. This software could also be a specialist app to solve a particular problem. For instance, the popular Microsoft Company designed Microsoft Word to solve the problem of word documentation. The

software could sell for as much as $100 per sale. Even a time-wasting app such as games you can play on systems or phones can earn the producer a huge amount of money. A side project could be purchased by big-tech Companies and could make the producer of such software super-rich in split seconds. Independent developers made $20 billion in the App Store in 2016 alone.

5. **E-commerce site**: setting up a virtual shop to sell physical items is one of the oldest and most time-tested ways of making a lot of money on the internet. Nowadays, the internet has made this line of business super cool and easy. Online sites like Shopify have made it easier than ever to create an amazing and powerful e-commerce site and commence selling of physical products digitally.

To make easily make money via this network, you need to create a niche that people would love to buy from. Secondly, you have to purchase cost-friendly goods manufactured in foreign countries like China, USA, and England. Then, repackage and combine these goods with other ones and sell them for better and higher prices.

6. **Becoming an Expert**: similar to selling your freelancing services online, you can also start selling your knowledge in a niche you are proficient in either as a coach or a consultant. If you can distinguish yourself as a proven expert, there are millionaire people on the internet ready to pay for your services. Being an online coach or consultant is a great way to make money simply by selling your expertise. Plus, online tutoring or teaching is a great way to build an

online business. More so, if you can distinctively set yourself as an Online tutor and compress your knowledge and expertise into an easily decipherable course, you are the trail of making it significantly in this business model. Now, to make money easily on this network, you have to discover your audience – persons who need your expertise. Online networks like Clarity.fm, Udemy, and Coach.me provide you with a network of potential clients to sell your expertise. As a specialist, one of the fastest means of generating revenue online is through selling your expertise via online courses communities.

7. **Owning a YouTube Channel**: arguably, YouTube is one of the largest search engines and the third most-visited site in the world. In 2017, it was recorded that over 5 billion videos were watched on YouTube every

single day. Even though in recent times, YouTube has made it monetization program more strident, if you can consistently hit 1,000 subscribers and 4,000 hours of view, it is an incredible channel to make cool cash remotely. On YouTube, the more views you get, the more earnings you make. In 2020, YouTube has been acclaimed as one of the fastest-growing networks you can make money with. Becoming a professional YouTube user is a lot like becoming a professional blog owner, except that you are working on a video – not writing. In the overall sense, there are two trendy niches on YouTube – the entertainment niche and the educational niche. Hence, to maximize your earning as a user on YouTube, you have to choose a niche, set up and build your channel on YouTube. Upon actualization of those mentioned above, you can go ahead to develop your subscribers' community. More subscribers mean more views which in turn earns you more money.

8. **E-book Publishing**: for those extremely gifted with the creative skill of writing and dream of writing a book, publishing your write-up as an e-book is an excellent idea. By packaging your ideas into a downloadable e-book is a great way to go about earning via e-book publishing. Your e-book could be in the form of a career advancement note, teaching transferrable skills, teaching people how to go about start-up or books on self-help. Bear in mind, however, that the more value your book exudes, the higher the probability that people would buy your books, which in turn would increase your earnings. Now, having written a book, you need an online platform you

publish on. You can employ an easy tool such as Sellfy in order to sell your pdf books to interested readers quickly. Better still, you can even employ the use of the world's largest bookseller: Amazon, to publish your downloadable pdf. One interesting thing about self-publishing on Amazon is that you set your price, retain the rights to your book, and get premium access to Amazon's fleet of audience. On every sale, you take 70% while Amazon retains the rest as fees for publishing on their network.

9. **Renting your extra rooms or cars**: Getaround and Airbnb are acclaimed networks for sharing either your cars or extra space to unknown person – strangers. Weird, right? But the truth is, it is a great way to make good money online. For Airbnb, all you've to do to make money via this network is to up your free rooms

or space up on the network. Interestingly, membership on this network is completely free. To earn via Airbnb, all that is required of you to do is to: enroll your free or extra space on their website, then you decide the host you want to accommodate, input the price of your choice, and then once your listing is live, qualified guests (clients/host) can reach out to you. On Airbnb, users could potentially earn over $1000 every month. One unique feature of Airbnb is that it gives full discretionary power to the host party to provide pre-requisites and take in only clients that fit these pre-requisites. Also, a traveler or client usually get to see where they would stay online, and in the situation that what the clients saw online does not match what they see in person, plans to cancel such placement are also in place for such tourist/traveler (client).The network also guarantees an insurance policy for its members and also proffer that its members have an insurance policy against any sort of damages to their homes.

Also, to earn incomes on Getaround, the first and most crucial step is to log in to the Getaround website and create a Getaround account. At the moment, it is of imperative importance to sign up on Getaround through a Facebook account. Having signed up as a user, Getaround rents your car to a client, and you earn as much as $90 per trip (depending on the distance of the journey). However, I must state that becoming a member of Getaround requires the payment of a token before you can be a certified member.

CHAPTER FOUR: BECOMING A SUCCESSFUL REMOTE WORKER IN 2020

As I have highlighted earlier, working from home or any remote location of your choice, whilst also determining your schedule and being self-employed, is the new career path since the emergence of the Internet (World Wide Web). While agreeing that not all remote jobs are online jobs, an online career is a lot easier and requires little or no capital to start – all thanks to the internet. This chapter – the final chapter shall further enlighten you with practicable and practical steps to take to become a successful remote worker.

1. **You need to find a niche that fits your person**: for

every person in the universe, there is a thing you find immense pleasure doing. There is something for every man. Something he can create magic from effortlessly. For instance, Ethan might be someone who finds creating graphics designing pretty easy whilst Reginald can effortlessly create 3D animations in seconds. So, the first step is to take in becoming a successful remote worker – is finding your place of interest – your niche. As soon as you discover this, your remote job career becomes effectual, and you would surely perform maximally and optimally at work.

2. **Joining the right remote job network**: having discovered a niche that works for work for you, there is a need to search for persons (clients) who are interested in paying for your services. For instance, for a freelance writer or copywriter – visiting websites like

Fiverr, Upwork or Freelancer is a perfect approach to finding clients that would pay for their services. Also, for those planning to monetize their blog, they can go about it in several ways. First, you can either use the WordPress option or blogger, which is a commercial-free platform. So, for a blogger – you earn by putting up adverts on your blog site and then charge clients for it. The WordPress domain is an excellent website for a jolly-just-come blogger. Also, network like – InboxDollars, Fancy Hands amongst other Digital side gigs network pays virtual assistants to perform mini-tasks online without charging a cent to sign up. These mini-tasks could include online research answering emails, booking travel, making appointments, data entry, inter alia. For these mini-tasks, these networks pay as much as $3.00 - $5.00 for newbies and the pay increases as you go up from being a rookie to becoming a professional.

3. **Improve yourself**: as a remote worker, there is a pertinent need to improve your current skills and acquire new ones. On platforms like Freelancer, Fiverr and Hubspot, users can acquire new skills that distinguish them from other remote workers. The point is, there are several remote workers out there, so, the more you improve your skills, earn certifications and acquire new licenses, the better for you. As the higher your skills certifications and licenses, the greater your chances are when you bid for jobs with fellow remote workers. Also, clients pay remote workers who have distinguished themselves either in terms of years of experience or by virtual of the skills, licenses and certification better than those who

possess little or none of these qualities.

4. **Feedbacks from clients**: another thing that is pivotal to the success of a remote worker is, excellent feedbacks from clients you have once worked for. Clients like to see that the person that they are giving their jobs to is credible and reliable. And credibility can be easily earned by lovely comments from former clients. Bear in mind, however, that these lovely comments can only be earned from clients that you have done an incredible job for. Hence, the cycle is such that: you do an impeccable job for a client, then he or she gives you excellent reviews which in turn earns more jobs, even with bigger and better pay. On some remote job sites, they even go as far as giving their remote workers star, and you can only earn these stars through wonderful review from clients you have

worked for. Even in the corporate world, it is not unknown that a job well done for a client makes a client refer the doer of the job to another person who wants to contract for the same job.

5. **Understanding your clients**: make sure you understand what your clients expect of you, and as a creative, you have to remodel their initiatives into yours completely. For instance, if a mourning mother employs your services to write a book in honor of her dead son. It is not unexpected that a remote freelance writer has to soak himself completely into the state of the woman to understand how she feels and communicate her feelings the way she would express it if she had written the book herself. So, to become a successful remote worker, you need to understand your client, his or her needs, what they want, and how

they want. Your client's satisfaction should be your top priority.

6. **Designate a separate workspace for yourself and take a regular break from work**: a remote worker needs to designate a particular space where he or she works. It could use your home library, the public library, the coffee shop or even your bedroom. The most important thing is that you can work maximally and optimally from any of these places. Separating business place from personal space can also help you focus better and work with little or no distractions either from family members or friends.

Taking regular breaks from work is also essential for a remote worker. Since you're working remotely and with little or no distractions – you may end staring at your computer for long or sitting on a spot for long and ending up with a backache or eye ache. At every hour, you need to take a break from being sedent and either take a coffee break or receive some fresh air. Taking a break from work allows you to refresh and get better and be more productive with your work.

CHAPTER FIVE: KNOWING WHAT REMOTE EMPLOYERS WANT

If you've been surfing the internet and searching for remote jobs, you would have noticed that there are some household companies and employers when it comes to remote works. Another significant thing you would have observed is: while some remote jobs are full-time, some others are part-time.

As an applicant seeking remote jobs, you don't care if the job is full-time or part-time, as long the position you applied for is remote, you immediately jump at the offer. Half the battle of landing a remote job is knowing where to look, and knowing what these remote employers are looking for. Unarguably, every employer

– remote or not – require two things from applicants or intending workers. These two things are:

- **Trustworthiness and ability to keep up with deadlines**: remote employers need to be able to trust their workers to do their jobs and deliver top-notch, high-quality and premium work. One crucial reason why remote employers don't mingle with an untrustworthy person is that – micromanagement is impossible in remote jobs. The company cannot closely supervise or monitor their workers until the job is completely done. Don't be astonished when you land your first remote job interview and all the interviewer wants to talk about is your trustworthiness and how you can work with little or no supervision. Before you decide to become a remote worker, you must put into consideration one thing – the ability to deliver premium works with low or zero control. The possession of this ability automatically make you a hot-cake for remote employees, and they find you trustworthy quickly. Most remote hiring managers are highly intelligent emotionally. They almost always can tell if you are genuine or not. So the best advice I can give for someone applying for remote work is that he/she acts like him or herself as doing this make you look trustworthy and genuine. Another trait – a very pertinent characteristic – required of a remote worker (employee) is the ability to keep to deadlines. As much as your earning are important, keeping to your deadlines is to the remote employers. In a survey recently carried out, it was observed one of the most prevalent reasons why remote employers relieve their worker of their jobs, is because of the remote employee's inability to stay faithful to deadlines.

- **Professionalism and immeasurable love for the job**: as pertinent as hiring a trustworthy person is a to a hiring manager, so also is – hiring a professional who shows that he is passionate about what he does. This might break your heart, but if you are applying for a remote job solely because you hate your work and you feel that working from home would help, I am sorry to announce to you that it won't. Working remotely even makes it worse. As working from home comes with a plethora of beautiful distractions. There is your TV to distract you in the morning. There are your kids to deal with in the afternoon and probably your dog or pet in the night. If you don't love your job or have passion for what you do while you had co-workers and bosses, you most likely won't still be passionate when you are left alone to work all by yourself. Respectfully, working from home or remotely is reserved for highly-motivated individuals who are passionate about their jobs. Harsh? Forgive me. But I just had to spill the bitter truth. Acclaimed remote employees would surely agree with me on this, as you don't need to master the encyclopedia to know that – as a remote worker you need to get your motivators to be in the right places at all times.

Also, as a remote worker showing professionalism at work requires that you develop yourself well to be a problem solver. Remote employers love their employees to be versatile and be capable of solving problems on their own. The reason for this is not far-fetched. Since you work remotely, your employer might be at your beck-and-call all the time. So anytime you can't reach your employer, and you have a problem, it is expected of you to solve these problems by yourself. Remote companies are specifically always on the look-out for independent workers. While preparing for a remote job interview, you need to prepare to speak about your independent work experience.

CHAPTER SIX: CRAFTING YOUR RESUME FOR A REMOTE JOB

At this juncture, you need to understanding that your resume is what will land you an interview with a remote job hiring manager. Also, your resume is the first impression a remote hiring manager has of you. And you know what they said about first impressions – they last forever. Below, I would be highlighting a few things you need to include in your resume. These steps would make your resume stand out exceptionally among other resume submitted by fellow remote job seekers for the same job and the same remote company or client.

Be a good communicator: your communication with the remote hiring manager starts on your resume. From your resume, a remote worker must be able to decipher that you can express yourself fluently and freely. Your resume must portray your communication skills, and you must completely flee from typographical errors as they tend to piss remote hiring mangers off.

Location: surprised? Yes, remote jobs like I mentioned earlier are not wholly online jobs. So, those that are not online-based are location specific. Sven though some online remote jobs are location-specific too. Nevertheless, it is essential for your location clearly in your resume.

Talk about tools: remote companies use software to bridge the communication gap. Ergo, you need to list any software tool you are abreast with on your resume.

Some of such tool may include but are not restricted to: Skype, Hangouts, Zapier, Zoom, Google Hangout, GoToMeeting, etc.

Display of Independence: also, your resume should demonstrate and show the hiring manager that you are an independent person who can work productively and optimally with little or zero supervision. To illustrate this, you simply just have to income on your resume tasks and projects you have carried out in the past with little or no supervision. Your ability to deliver a premium job with little or no supervision is an eye-catching part of your resume that the hiring manager wouldn't treat with levity.

Result-oriented and a problem solver: if you had achieved several things maybe while working at your former remote company, it is a massive plus for you when you include that in your resume. For instance, if you have marketing skills that helped improved the traffic on X company's website while you were a copywriter with them – that's a piece of incredible resume information. You shouldn't leave that out. Also, on your resume, you must be able to convincingly show the hiring manager that you are a highly-motivated individual who also doubles as a problem solver.

CONCLUSION

Remote works are focused-based jobs. They are also result-oriented. Remote companies are on the look-out for an individual whose deliverables are top-notch, premium and of high-quality. For remote job seekers, this book has outlined what remote jobs are, the types of remote jobs available in 2020, where and how to find them. Additionally, the book also served as an eye-opener to develop from being a rookie remote worker to being a professional remote worker. In this book, an outline of what remote employers are looking for was given. Also, how to craft an eye-catching resume that would land you your first remote job with the remote desire company of yours was also discussed. For those that might like a recap, here is one:

- Remote work is also a style of working which allows professionals to work outside the typical office environment.
- Remote jobs are solely freelancing jobs
- The benefits of remote jobs. For me, the most important one is the flexibility that comes with the job.
- The best sites for remote job hunting was also discussed.
- Understanding what remote job employers require of remote job seekers was also expounded on.
- The indelible traits of a remote worker: Trustworthiness and passion for one's job
- Preparing the perfect resume for remote job

applications

Good luck with landing those remote jobs you desire so dearly. I hope you had a lovely time reading as I had while writing. For your time, I say thank you!

Made in the USA
Middletown, DE
04 July 2020